Mommy, Is Today Sabbath?

This book is dedicated to
Marcus,
whose question inspired the story.

All scriptures taken from the King James Version
unless otherwise noted.

Jacqueline Galloway-Blake

Artwork by Max Stasuyk

Copyright © 2012 TEACH Services, Inc.
ISBN-13: 978-1-57258-544-7 (Paperback)
ISBN-13: 978-1-57258-910-0 (ePub)
ISBN-13: 978-1-57258-911-7 (Kindle)
Library of Congress Control Number: 2012946386

TEACH Services, Inc.
P U B L I S H I N G
www.TEACHServices.com

Mommy, is today Sabbath?
No, son, today is Sunday,
your trip day.
Get ready, let's go to the zoo
and see the animals
God made for you.

Mommy, is today Sabbath?
No, son, today is Monday,
my wash day.
Help me sort the laundry, light and dark.
Then we'll wash, dry and fold
and you can do your part.

Mommy, is today Sabbath?
No, son, today is Tuesday,
helping day.
We'll find someone in the neighborhood
who needs a helping hand.
Let's rake Mrs. Coleman's yard.
She's crippled and can't stand.

Mommy, is today Sabbath?
No, son, today is Wednesday,
library day.
We'll take a look at lots of books
about panda bears, airplanes and trees.
Then listen during the story hour
to the librarian as she reads.

Mommy, is today Sabbath?
No, son, today is Thursday,
baking day.
Let's bake raisin bread,
     you knead the dough.
Then stir the cake batter—
     in the oven they go.

Mommy, is today Sabbath?
No, son, today is Friday,
preparation day.
Hand me the lace tablecloth,
candles and plates.
The house is clean, we're ready.
There's Daddy, please open the gate.

Mommy, is today Sabbath?
Yes, son, today is Sabbath,
the best day.
You waited patiently.
Now let's count the days
of the week and see
1-2-3-4-5-6-7.

The 7th day is Sabbath,
God's special day He blessed.
The Sabbath day is better
than all the rest!

How many groups of 7 can you find in this picture?
Did you find at least five?

Yeah!
We'll sing and pray at church today,
then come home for a special treat.

Mommy, I really love the Sabbath and can't wait for it to come again next week!

Review

Day

1... Sunday .... Trip Day

2... Monday .... Wash Day

3... Tuesday .... Helping Day

4... Wednesday .... Library Day

5... Thursday .... Baking Day

6... Friday .... Preparation Day

7... SABBATH .... God's Special Day

Can you put the days of the week in order?
Write a number next to each day.
Place a "star" next to God's holy day

Wednesday   _____

Monday   _____

Saturday   _____

Sunday   _____

Thursday   _____

Tuesday   _____

Friday   _____

Draw a design using the seven days of the week.

Questions for Children

1. Can you name the days of the week? _____

_____

2. Which day do you like best? Why? _____

_____

3. What do *you* do on the other days? _____

_____

4. How do you help to prepare (get ready) for the Sabbath? _____

_____

5. Do you like the Sabbath? Why? _____

_____

6. What do you like to do on the Sabbath day? _____

_____

7. What did God do to make the Sabbath a happy day? _____

_____

Draw a picture about the Sabbath

Questions for Parents

1. Listen to your child's answers to the questions.

2. Is the Sabbath a joy for your child? Is it eagerly anticipated as in the story?

3. If not, what can you do to make the Sabbath a "day of delight" for your child?

_____

_____

_____

_____

_____

A Bible Promise

"If thou turn away thy foot from the Sabbath, from doing thy pleasure on my holy day, and call the Sabbath <u>a delight</u>, the holy of the Lord, honourable; and shalt honour him, not doing thine own ways nor finding thine own pleasure, nor speaking thine own words: then shalt thou <u>delight</u> thyself in the Lord; and I will cause thee to ride upon the high places of the earth, and feed thee with the heritage of Jacob thy father; for the mouth of the Lord hath spoken it." —Isaiah 58: 13, 14

Bible Texts

Preparation Day (day before Sabbath)

"And now when the even was come, because it was the preparation, that is, the day before the sabbath." —Mark 15:42

"And the day was the preparation, and the sabbath drew on." —Luke 23:54

Sabbath Day

"Now the next day, that followed the day of the preparation, the chief priests and Pharisees came together unto Pilate." —Matthew 27:62

"And they returned, and prepared spices and ointments; and rested the sabbath day according to the commandment." —Luke 23:56

"Remember the Sabbath day, to keep it holy. Six days shalt thou labour and do all thy work: but the seventh day is the Sabbath of the Lord thy God......for in six days the Lord made heaven and earth, the sea, and all that in them is, and rested the seventh day: wherefore the Lord blessed the sabbath day, and hallowed it." —Exodus 20: 8-11

"And God blessed the seventh day, and sanctified it: because that in it he had rested from all his work which God created and made." —Genesis 2:3

"And he came to Nazareth, where he had been brought up: and, as his custom was, he went into the synagogue on the sabbath day, and stood up for to read."—Luke 4:16

First Day (day after Sabbath)

"In the end of the sabbath, as it began to dawn toward the first day of the week, came Mary Magdalene and the other Mary to see the sepulchre." —Matthew 28:1

"Now when Jesus was risen early the first day of the week, he appeared first to Mary Magdalene, out of whom he had cast seven devils." —Mark 16:9

"Now upon the first day of the week, very early in the morning, they came unto the sepulchre, bringing the spices which they had prepared, and certain others with them." —Luke 24:1

Paste Photo Here

My name is

Skylar

I am ___4___ years old

and I love Sabbath, too!